Hey Beautiful

Learning to See Yourself Through God's Eyes

Dr. LaTonia Harrell

Printed in the United States of America.

Dedication

To my daughters Audreanna, Taneah, Kalyn and LaTonia always remember that you are beautiful.

To my granddaughters Amiah and Ah'Neah you are a beautiful blessing.

To every girl who has ever questioned her worth.

To every young woman learning who she is in a noisy world.

To every woman who has carried pain quietly while still showing up for others.

This book is for the one who felt unseen, unheard, or misunderstood.

For the one who learned to be strong before she ever learned to rest.

For the one still healing, still hoping, still becoming.

May these pages remind you that you are not broken — you are becoming.

May you see yourself the way God has always seen you: chosen, loved, and deeply valued.

Hey Beautiful, this is for you.

Contents

How to Use This Book

This book is both a devotional and a guided journal.

Each chapter includes:

- A faith-based reflection
- A Scripture reference (NLT)
- A short prayer
- Reflection questions
- Structured journaling pages

You may read one chapter a day, one a week, or return to any section as needed.

There is no rush. Healing and growth happen at God's pace.

Take your time. Reflect honestly. Write freely.

This space is safe.

Introduction

Before You Turn the Page

Hey Beautiful,

Before anyone told you who to be, God already knew who you were. Before comparison crept in, before fear spoke loudly, before life tried to label you, heaven had already spoken your name.

This book is a gentle mirror. Not one that reflects flaws, but one that reflects truth.

It is a reminder that your value is not earned, negotiated, or taken away. It is given — freely and lovingly — by God.

You don't have to fix yourself to be worthy.

You don't have to perform to be loved.

You don't have to wait to belong.

You already do.

As you turn these pages, allow yourself to slow down. Let Scripture speak. Let truth replace lies. Let healing begin where you may have once hidden pain.

This is not about becoming someone new.

It is about remembering who you have always been in God's eyes.

You are seen.

You are known.

You are deeply loved.

Turn the page.

Your becoming continues here.

Part I
Seeing Yourself Clearly

Chapter 1
You Were Seen First

Hey Beautiful,

Before you ever took your first breath, God already knew your name. Before anyone formed an opinion about you, heaven had already decided your worth. You were not created by accident or oversight — you were formed with intention, care, and deep love.

There will be moments in life when you feel overlooked, unheard, or unseen. Seasons where it seems like everyone else is being chosen while you wait quietly on the sidelines. But God has never confused your place or forgotten your presence. His eyes have always been on you.

Being seen by God does not mean life will always feel easy. It means you are never alone in it. He sees your tears, your questions, your silent prayers, and even the parts of you that you try to hide. And He does not turn away.

He sees you — fully — and loves you completely.

Scripture

Psalm 139:1–4 (NLT)

Prayer

God, thank You for seeing me completely. When I feel overlooked or forgotten, remind me that I have never been invisible to You. Help me rest in the truth that I am known and deeply loved. Amen.

Reflection

1. When have I recently felt unseen or overlooked?

2. What does it mean to me that God knows my thoughts and heart?
3. Where do I need to rest in the truth that I am fully known and loved?

JOURNAL

Chapter 2
You Are Not What Happened to You

Hey Beautiful,

Life has a way of trying to rename us.

Sometimes it is a mistake.

Sometimes it is a failure.

Sometimes it is something painful we did not choose.

But what happened to you is not who you are.

You may have experienced rejection, disappointment, heartbreak, betrayal, or loss.

You may carry memories that still sting when you think about them. But those experiences do not get to define your identity.

Pain is something you walk through — not something you become.

God does not introduce you by your worst day. He does not call you by your lowest moment. He does not see you through the lens of what hurt you.

He sees who you are becoming.

Healing does not erase the past. It restores your perspective about it. It reminds you that what tried to break you did not get the final word.

Your story includes pain — but it does not end there.

You are more than your scars.

You are more than your struggle.

You are more than what happened.

Scripture

Isaiah 43:18–19 (NLT)

Prayer

God, help me separate my identity from my experiences. Teach me to see myself the way You do — not defined by pain, but shaped by purpose. Amen.

Reflection

1. What past experience has tried to define me?
2. How has God shown faithfulness even in difficult seasons?
3. What truth do I need to speak over myself today?

JOURNAL

Chapter 3

Comparison Is a Thief

Hey Beautiful,

Comparison is quiet, but it is powerful.

It does not always announce itself loudly. Sometimes it slips in subtly — through scrolling, conversations, or even internal thoughts you did not realize were forming. It whispers that you should be further, doing more, looking different, achieving faster.

And slowly, it steals.

It steals joy.

It steals contentment.

It steals confidence.

Comparison convinces you that someone else's highlight reel is the standard for your real life. It tempts you to measure your progress against someone else's pace.

But God never asked you to run their race.

He gave you your own.

Your timeline is not delayed.

Your growth is not behind.

Your journey is not inferior.

Different does not mean deficient.

When you focus too long on what someone else is building, you can lose sight of what God is building in you. And what He is building in you is intentional.

Stay in your lane.

Honor your process.

Trust your becoming.

There is space for you.

There is purpose for you.

There is enough for you.

Scripture

Galatians 6:4 (NLT)

Prayer

God, help me silence comparison. Teach me to celebrate others without diminishing myself. Anchor my heart in gratitude for the path You have given me. Amen.

Reflection

1. Where has comparison recently stolen my joy?
2. What unique strengths has God placed in me?
3. How can I celebrate my own growth this week?

JOURNAL

Part II

Chapter 4
It's Okay to Heal Slowly

Hey Beautiful,

Healing is not a race.

Some wounds close quickly. Others take time. And sometimes the deeper the hurt, the longer the restoration. But slow healing is still healing.

The world often pressures you to "move on" quickly. To be strong. To bounce back. To pretend that everything is fine. But God does not rush restoration. He works gently and intentionally.

Healing is not weakness.

It is courage.

It takes bravery to sit with pain instead of burying it. It takes strength to face what hurt you instead of pretending it didn't matter.

God is not frustrated by your pace. He is present in your process.

You are allowed to grieve.

You are allowed to pause.

You are allowed to take your time.

There is no expiration date on becoming whole.

What matters is not how fast you heal — but that you do.

Scripture

Psalm 147:3 (NLT)

Prayer

God, give me patience in my healing. Remind me that restoration is a journey, not an event. Help me trust that You are working even when progress feels slow. Amen.

Reflection

1. Where am I pressuring myself to heal faster?
2. What part of my story still needs gentle attention?
3. How can I show myself grace this week?

JOURNAL

Chapter 5

Releasing What Weighs You Down

Hey Beautiful,

There are things we carry that were never meant to stay.

Old guilt.

Old shame.

Old conversations replayed in our minds.

Old expectations we can never seem to meet.

Sometimes the weight becomes so familiar that we forget what it feels like to walk freely.

But freedom begins with release.

God never intended for you to carry burdens that He already offered to lift. When you hold on to what He has invited you to surrender, exhaustion follows.

Releasing does not mean pretending something did not matter. It means deciding it no longer controls you.

You cannot move fully into your next season while dragging pieces of the past behind you.

Let go of what no longer serves your growth.

Let go of words spoken over you that were never true.

Let go of the need to fix everything yourself.

God is strong enough to hold what you release.

And you are strong enough to let it go.

Scripture

Matthew 11:28–30 (NLT)

Prayer

God, help me release what has been weighing on my heart. Teach me to surrender burdens I was never meant to carry. Replace heaviness with peace. Amen.

Reflection

1. What emotional weight am I still carrying?
2. Why have I been hesitant to release it?
3. What would freedom look like for me?

JOURNAL

Chapter 6

Grace for the Girl You Used to Be

Hey Beautiful,

There was a version of you who didn't know what you know now.

She made decisions with limited understanding.

She trusted people she shouldn't have.

She reacted from wounds she hadn't healed yet.

And she deserves grace.

It is easy to look back and criticize who you used to be. To replay moments and wish you had responded differently. To carry regret like it is still required.

But growth means you have changed.

You are not the same girl.

You have learned.

You have matured.

You have healed.

The fact that you see things differently now is proof that God has been working in you.

Do not shame your past self for surviving the best way she knew how.

Honor her.

She got you here.

Grace is not just something you extend to others. It is something you must extend to yourself.

You are allowed to forgive yourself.

You are allowed to move forward.

You are allowed to evolve.

God does not hold your past over your head. He uses it to shape your future.

Scripture

Romans 8:1 (NLT)

Prayer

God, help me extend grace to the girl I used to be. Free me from regret and remind me that I am growing, not stuck. Thank You for never giving up on me. Amen.

Reflection

1. What part of my past do I still criticize myself for?
2. How have I grown since then?
3. What would it look like to forgive myself fully?

JOURNAL

Part III
Becoming with God

Chapter 7
Growing Without Rushing

Hey Beautiful,

You are not late.

You are not behind.

You are not failing because your journey looks different from someone else's.

Growth with God is never rushed. Becoming takes time.

We live in a world that celebrates speed — quick success, instant results, overnight transformation. But God often chooses process over pressure. He grows us slowly, deeply, and intentionally so that what He builds in us lasts.

There are seasons when growth feels quiet. No applause. No obvious milestones. Just steady faithfulness. Those seasons matter more than you know. Roots are forming beneath the surface even when nothing seems to be happening above ground.

The world may ask, "Why aren't you further?"

But God asks, "Are you becoming?"

Progress in the Kingdom is not measured by visibility. It is measured by obedience.

Give yourself permission to grow at God's pace. He is not disappointed in your progress. He is not frustrated by your process. He is walking with you through it.

Slow growth is still growth.

And what grows slowly often grows strong.

Scripture

Ecclesiastes 3:1 (NLT)

Prayer

God, help me trust the season I'm in. Teach me to resist the urge to rush what You are still shaping. Give me patience with myself and confidence in Your timing. Amen.

Reflection

1. Where do I feel pressure to move faster than I should?
2. What might God be growing in me beneath the surface?
3. How can I embrace this season instead of resisting it?

JOURNAL

Chapter 8
Confidence Rooted in Christ

Hey Beautiful,

Confidence doesn't come from having it all together — it comes from knowing who holds you together.

The world often defines confidence as loudness, perfection, or constant achievement. But biblical confidence is different. It is quiet assurance. It is steady trust. It is knowing that even when you feel weak, God's strength is still working within you.

Confidence rooted in Christ is not shaken by opinions, mistakes, or setbacks. It does not rise and fall with compliments or criticism. It remains steady because its source is steady.

When your identity is anchored in Christ, you do not have to prove yourself to anyone. You do not have to shrink to make others comfortable. You do not have to overperform to feel secure.

God already knows what He placed inside of you.

And He delights in helping you grow into it.

There will be days when doubt tries to creep in. When insecurity whispers that you are not enough. In those moments, remember this: your confidence is not built on your ability — it is built on God's faithfulness.

And He does not fail.

Confidence rooted in Christ does not say, "I can do anything on my own."

It says, "With God, I am strengthened."

That kind of confidence lasts.

Scripture

Philippians 4:13 (NLT)

Prayer

Lord, help me place my confidence in You instead of in my performance. When doubt tries to overwhelm me, remind me that Your strength is enough. Teach me to walk with steady assurance rooted in who You are. Amen.

Reflection

1. Where have I been placing my confidence lately?
2. What situations tend to shake my sense of security?
3. How can I anchor my identity more deeply in Christ this season?

JOURNAL

Chapter 9

Learning to Love Yourself Well

Hey Beautiful,

Learning to love yourself is not a switch you flip overnight. It is a journey.

For many women, loving others comes naturally. You encourage. You show up. You forgive. You extend grace. But when it comes to yourself, the tone changes. The words become harsher. The expectations become heavier.

You replay mistakes.

You magnify flaws.

You hold yourself to standards you would never require of someone you love.

God invites you into a better way.

Loving yourself well does not mean ignoring growth or pretending everything is perfect. It means allowing grace to walk alongside growth. It means seeing yourself through the same compassionate lens that God uses.

You are not your worst moment.

You are not your past mistake.

You are not defined by what you wish you had done differently.

When Jesus said to love your neighbor as yourself, it assumed something important — that you would care for yourself too.

Self-love rooted in God is not pride. It is stewardship. It is recognizing that your heart, mind, and body are precious gifts entrusted to you.

Speak to yourself with kindness.

Rest without guilt.

Set boundaries without apology.

Forgive yourself without hesitation.

The way you treat yourself matters.

And you are worthy of gentle care.

Scripture

Mark 12:31 (NLT)

Prayer

God, teach me how to love myself in a healthy and grace-filled way. Help me release self-criticism and replace it with truth. Show me how to care for my heart as something valuable in Your sight. Amen.

Reflection

1. In what ways have I been overly critical of myself?
2. How would my life change if I treated myself with more compassion?
3. What practical step can I take this week to care for myself well?

JOURNAL

Part IV
Walking in Purpose

Chapter 10
Created for More Than Survival

Hey Beautiful,

You were never created just to make it through the day.

God did not breathe life into you so that you could live exhausted, discouraged, or disconnected from hope. Even if there were seasons where survival was necessary, it was never meant to be the destination.

There are moments when life demands everything you have — when you are simply holding on, praying quietly, and doing the best you can. If that has been you, hear this clearly: surviving does not mean you lack faith. It means you are human.

And God meets you right there.

But God's heart for you stretches beyond endurance. He invites you to lift your eyes and imagine more — more peace, more joy, more purpose. Not overnight. Not all at once. But step by step.

Thriving with God does not mean a life without struggle. It means a life filled with meaning even in the struggle.

You still have permission to dream.

You still have permission to hope again.

You still have permission to believe that better days are ahead.

Your story is not over.

Your purpose is not exhausted.

Your life carries more than survival.

It carries calling.

And calling grows when you trust God with the next step.

Scripture

Jeremiah 29:11 (NLT)

Prayer

God, when I feel tired or stuck in survival mode, remind me that You have more for me. Help me lift my eyes toward hope and trust that my purpose is still unfolding. Amen.

Reflection

1. Where have I been living in survival instead of purpose?
2. What dream or hope have I quietly put aside?
3. What small step can I take toward thriving again?

JOURNAL

Chapter 11
Trusting God with the Unknown

Hey Beautiful,

The unknown can feel unsettling.

Not knowing what comes next can stir fear, doubt, and endless questions. We like plans. We like clarity. We like timelines that make sense. But faith often asks us to walk without all the answers.

Trusting God does not mean pretending you aren't afraid. It means choosing to place your confidence in Him even when your path feels unclear.

You may not know how everything will work out.

You may not see the full picture.

You may not understand the timing.

But God does.

When the future feels uncertain, remember that God already stands in it. He sees what you cannot see. He prepares what you cannot predict. He works in ways you may not immediately recognize.

The same God who guided you before will guide you again.

The same God who carried you through past seasons will carry you forward.

You are not lost.

You are being led.

Trust grows when control loosens. Peace rises when surrender replaces striving. And sometimes the greatest growth happens when you release your need to understand everything.

You do not need to know every detail.

You only need to trust the One who does.

Scripture

Proverbs 3:5–6 (NLT)

Prayer

God, help me release my need for control. When I feel anxious about what lies ahead, remind me that You are already there. Strengthen my trust and quiet my uncertainty. Amen.

Reflection

1. What unknown situation is causing me the most anxiety right now?
2. Where am I trying to control outcomes instead of trusting God?
3. What would surrender look like in this season?

JOURNAL

Chapter 12
Becoming Bold in Faith

Hey Beautiful,

Bold faith does not mean you never feel afraid. It means you choose to trust God even when fear tries to hold you back.

Becoming bold is a process. It often begins quietly — with small steps of obedience that no one else sees. A prayer whispered when doubt creeps in. A boundary set when it would be easier to stay silent. A decision made even when the outcome is unclear.

There will be moments when God invites you to step outside what feels familiar. To speak when you would rather stay quiet. To believe when circumstances suggest otherwise.

Bold faith is not about having all the answers.

It is about knowing who you are walking with.

God is not asking you to be fearless. He is asking you to be faithful.

Every time you choose trust over doubt, courage grows. Every time you take one step forward, your faith stretches stronger.

You do not have to be perfect to be bold. You just have to be willing.

God delights in using ordinary women to do extraordinary things through His power. Your obedience — even in small things — carries eternal impact.

Faith is not passive. It is active trust. It shows up in how you pray, how you respond, how you persevere.

And when you walk by faith, you are never walking alone.

Step forward.

He is with you.

Scripture

Hebrews 11:1 (NLT)

Prayer

God, help me step into bold faith. Give me courage to trust You even when the path feels uncertain. Strengthen my willingness to obey and remind me that You are walking with me every step of the way. Amen.

Reflection

1. Where is God inviting me to take a bold step of faith?
2. What fear do I need to surrender in order to move forward?
3. What small act of obedience can I take this week?

JOURNAL

Closing

A Letter to You

Hey Beautiful,

If you have made it to this point, pause for a moment.

Breathe.

Let this truth settle gently in your heart: you are still becoming — and that is not a flaw. It is a gift.

Growth is not instant. Healing is not linear. Faith is not always loud. But your willingness to continue — to read, to reflect, to pray — speaks volumes about the strength within you.

Every page you have read is evidence that you desire more.

More clarity.

More peace.

More alignment with who God created you to be.

And God honors that desire.

He meets you in your questions.

He steadies you in uncertainty.

He strengthens you in quiet ways that others may never see.

As you close this book, remember: this is not an ending.

It is an invitation.

An invitation to walk daily with God.

To speak life over yourself.

To guard your peace.

To choose faith again tomorrow.

You will still have moments of doubt. You will still face challenges. But you will face them differently now — anchored in truth.

When old thoughts try to return, remind yourself of what you have learned.

You are seen.
You are chosen.
You are healing.
You are becoming.
You are called.
And you are deeply loved.
Keep showing up.
Keep trusting.
Keep becoming.

Love and blessings,
Dr. LaTonia Harrell

Daily Hey Beautiful Affirmations

A 12-Day Reflection Journey

Read one affirmation each day.

Speak it aloud.

Write it again.

Let it take root.

DAY 1

Hey Beautiful, I am learning to see myself through God's eyes.

Reflection

DAY 2

Hey Beautiful, I am allowed to grow without rushing.

Reflection

DAY 3

Hey Beautiful, I am deeply loved and never alone.

Reflection

DAY 4

Hey Beautiful, my healing matters to God.

Reflection

DAY 5

Hey Beautiful, I am not behind — I am becoming.

Reflection

DAY 6

Hey Beautiful, God's grace meets me every day.

Reflection

DAY 7

Hey Beautiful, I do not have to earn my worth.

Reflection

DAY 8

Hey Beautiful, I can trust God with my future.

Reflection

DAY 9

Hey Beautiful, I am stronger than I think.

Reflection

DAY 10

Hey Beautiful, God is working even when I cannot see it.

Reflection

DAY 11

Hey Beautiful, I am chosen, called, and cared for.

Reflection

DAY 12

Hey Beautiful, my story is still unfolding.

Reflection

Scripture Reflections for Quiet Moments

Take one Scripture at a time.

Sit with it.

Read it slowly.

Journal honestly.

Psalm 139:14 (NLT)

What does being fearfully and wonderfully made mean for me today?

Isaiah 43:1 (NLT)

Where do I need to remember that I belong to God?

Jeremiah 29:11 (NLT)

What hope is God inviting me to trust?

Proverbs 3:5–6 (NLT)

What am I struggling to release control over?

Romans 8:1 (NLT)

What guilt or shame do I need to let go of?

Philippians 4:13 (NLT)

Where do I need God's strength right now?

A 30-Day Hey Beautiful Journey

Move through one day at a time.

There is no rush.

Let each truth settle deeply before moving forward.

DAY 1

God sees me. — Psalm 139:1

What does being seen mean to me today?

DAY 2

I am loved. — Romans 8:38–39

Where do I need to receive love?

DAY 3

I am becoming. — Philippians 1:6

What is God growing in me?

DAY 4

I can rest. — Matthew 11:28

What do I need to lay down?

DAY 5

I am not alone. — Deuteronomy 31:6

Where do I need reassurance?

DAY 6

I am chosen. — Ephesians 1:4

Where do I need confidence in being selected by God?

DAY 7

I release comparison. — Galatians 6:4

What joy can I reclaim today?

DAY 8

I walk in courage. — 2 Timothy 1:7

What fear do I need to surrender?

DAY 9

I trust God's timing. — Ecclesiastes 3:1

Where do I need patience?

DAY 10

My confidence is in Christ. — Philippians 4:13

What strengthens me most in this season?

DAY 11

I extend grace to myself. — Mark 12:31

How can I practice self-compassion today?

DAY 12

I am created with purpose. — Jeremiah 29:11

What dream is stirring again?

DAY 13

God guides my steps. — Proverbs 3:5–6

What decision do I need to trust Him with?

DAY 14

My faith is growing. — Hebrews 11:1

What bold step is God inviting me to take?

DAY 15

I am healed in progress. — Psalm 147:3

Where am I seeing signs of restoration?

DAY 16

I am deeply valued. — Matthew 10:29–31

Where have I forgotten my worth?

DAY 17

God is near to me. — James 4:8

How can I draw closer to Him today?

DAY 18

I am strong through God. — Isaiah 40:29

Where do I need renewed strength?

DAY 19

I am learning peace. — John 14:27

What anxiety can I surrender?

DAY 20

I am not defined by my past. — 2 Corinthians 5:17

What am I ready to release?

DAY 21

God is working behind the scenes. — Romans 8:28

Where do I need trust in unseen progress?

DAY 22

I am becoming wiser. — James 1:5

What insight do I need today?

DAY 23

I choose gratitude. — 1 Thessalonians 5:18

What can I thank God for right now?

DAY 24

I walk in obedience. — Joshua 1:9

What instruction do I need to follow?

DAY 25

I am anchored in hope. — Romans 15:13

Where do I need renewed hope?

DAY 26

I am fearfully and wonderfully made. — Psalm 139:14

What makes me uniquely designed?

DAY 27

God's mercy covers me. — Lamentations 3:22–23

Where do I need a fresh start?

DAY 28

I walk by faith. — 2 Corinthians 5:7

What uncertainty am I navigating?

DAY 29

I am strengthened daily. — Ephesians 3:16

Where do I feel growth within me?

DAY 30

My becoming continues. — Philippians 1:6

What is God still shaping in me?

Beautifully Unique

A Dedication to Those the World Misunderstands

Hey Beautiful,

To the ones the world tried to label.

To the ones who were called different.

Slow.

Too much.

Not enough.

To the ones who were told what they couldn't do before anyone ever discovered what they could do.

This space is for you.

The world may use the word "disabled."

But I choose a different word.

Unique.

Because every creation from God is intentional.

Every life is purposeful.

Every soul is handcrafted.

You are not a mistake.

You are not an accident.

You are not a flaw in the system.

You are wonderfully made.

Before anyone gave you a diagnosis,

God gave you destiny.

Before anyone formed an opinion,

God formed you.

Before the world spoke limitation,
He spoke life.
You are blessed.
You are highly favored.
You are carefully designed.
Your journey may look different.
But different does not mean deficient.
Different means divine design.
The world measures worth by speed, production, and performance.
God measures worth by purpose.
And purpose does not require perfection.
Some of the strongest spirits live in bodies the world underestimates.
Some of the brightest lights shine through what others misunderstand.
You are not behind.
You are not broken.
You are not forgotten.
You are seen.
There is beauty in how you think.
There is beauty in how you move.
There is beauty in how you express yourself.
You bring something to this earth that no one else can replicate.
That is not disability.
That is distinction.
If you have ever felt overlooked in rooms where you should have been celebrated, hear this clearly:
Your life carries weight.
Your presence carries power.
Your voice matters.
God does not create extras.
He creates essentials.
And you are essential.

May you walk boldly in who you are.
May you reject every label that tries to shrink you.
May you embrace the truth that you are blessed and highly favored.
You are not less than.
You are uniquely chosen.

Love and blessings,
Dr. LaTonia Harrell

About The Author

Dr. LaTonia Harrell is a licensed pastor, certified life coach, mentor, speaker, and nonprofit leader with over two decades of service to women, families, and communities. Through ministry, outreach, and personal development initiatives, she has dedicated her life to helping women discover their identity, heal from past wounds, and walk boldly in purpose.

She is the founder of Sisters Building Sisters Worldwide Ministries, a nonprofit organization committed to empowering women through faith, accountability, and authentic sisterhood.

Dr. Harrell holds an honorary Doctorate of Ministry in recognition of her community impact and leadership. Her passion is rooted in seeing women healed, whole, and anchored in God's truth.

She is a devoted wife, mother, grandmother, author, and encourager who believes that every woman deserves to see herself through God's eyes — not the world's expectations.

Final Journal Pages

Use these pages for continued reflection, prayer, and personal growth.
Let this space remain sacred.

www.ingramcontent.com/pod-product-compliance
Lightning Source LLC
LaVergne TN
LVHW010626100826
845148LV00014B/3135

* 9 7 9 8 2 3 4 0 2 1 1 6 8 *